READER'S DELIGHT

Biography of

MOTHER TERESA

READER'S DELIGHT
AN IMPRINT OF RAMESH PUBLISHING HOUSE
NEW DELHI

ISBN 978-93-5012-629-5

Published by: Alok Kumar Gupta *for* Reader's Delight
(An Imprint of Ramesh Publishing House)

Admin. Office: 12-H, New Daryaganj Road, Opp. Officers' Mess, New Delhi-110002 ✆ 23261567, 23275224, 23275124

Showroom: ● Balaji Market, Nai Sarak, Delhi-6 ✆ 23253720, 23282525

● 4457, Nai Sarak, Delhi-6 ✆ 23918938

E-Mail: info@rameshpublishinghouse.com
Website: www.rameshpublishinghouse.com

INDEMNIFICATION CLAUSE

- This book is being sold/distributed on the condition and understanding that the information given herein are merely for guidance and reference and must not be taken as authority, and neither the author nor the publishers individually or collectively, shall be responsible to indemnify the buyer/user/possessor of this book beyond the selling price of this book for any reason under any circumstances. If you do not agree to it, please do not buy/accept/use/possess this book.
- Though every care has been taken in printing this book, errors or ommissions might have crept inadvertently. The publishers shall be obliged if such error or ommission is brought to their notice.
- Subject to Delhi jurisdiction.

© *Publisher.*
No Part of this book may be reproduced or transmitted in any form or by any means, electronic or mechanical including photocopying, recording or by any transformation storage and retrieval system without prior permission from the Publisher.

A-28

*P*reface

The book provides excellent overview of Mother Teresa's beliefs, her noted humanistic works, and her vision to live and work among the poorest in the world.

In this biography, readers will follow Agnes Gonxha Bojaxhiu from her humble Mecidonian birth to worldwide celebrity as Mother Teresa. The nun who attended to the dying and diseased in Calcutta (now Kolkata), India, and established her Missionaries of Charity around the world, is revealed to have a singular determination from a young age.

Readers will be challenged to consider for themselves whether Mother Teresa deserves to be sainted. Mother Teresa is characterized as being ordinary and her life as mundane. The biography suggests that she transcended her ordinariness with a singular belief that she was called to life's work. When this work brought fame, which she never sought, she used it to further her causes.

In a global age, celebrity worship allowed her to work the system. She became an icon of service and selflessness, but her human flaws remained behind the saintliness.

Publisher

Contents

Introduction	5
Her Childhood	9
Life in the Slums	13
Mother in Kolkata	20
Beatification	25
Catholic Teachings	29
The Final Years	32
Awards	35
Words of the Mother	43
On Her Life's Work	54

INTRODUCTION

"The other day I dreamed that I was at the gates of heaven....and St. Peter said, 'Go back to Earth, there are no slums up here.'

- Mother Teresa

These words, once spoken by Mother Teresa, intensely recall the life of the late Roman Catholic nun and missionary known as *"the Saint of the Gutters."*

Mother Teresa devoted her life to the succour of the sick and the outcast. The earthly sufferers were nothing less than Christ in *"distressing disguise"* to her.

She is among the most well-known and highly respected women in the world in the latter half of the twentieth century. In 1948 she founded a religious order of nuns in Calcutta (now Kolkata), India, called the Missionaries of Charity.

She dedicated her life to helping the poor, the sick, and the dying around the world, particularly those in India.

She never got tired of the unlimited works she did for the slum people. Her selfless work with the needy brought her much acclaim and many awards, including the Nobel Peace Prize in 1979.

She was hardly a political figure in the conventional sense. But she had a politician's sense of issues and timing: she knew that in modern-day India, a nation of nearly a billion overwhelmingly poor people, the biggest issue of all was poverty.

She drew larger crowds and invited greater affection than any other politician. It proved the testimony to her integrity and her humility, qualities conspicuous by their absence in the men and women who govern the world's largest democracy today.

And like Mahatma Gandhi, Mother Teresa was an unelected spokesman for the poor everywhere—not simply highlighting their despair but also underscoring their hopes.

When she spoke, all India listened and the world took notice. No small feat that, especially when India's political stature has shrunk internationally in direct proportion to the growth of her social malaise and political corruption.

That is not to say Mother Teresa's judgement was unassailable on every issue. In a nation that adds 20 million people each year, more than the entire population of Australia, Mother Teresa stubbornly resisted family planning programmes. She was the Universal saviour of children.

In keeping with her conservative Catholic beliefs, she was vehemently opposed to abortion, which is permitted in India. She strongly advocated against the killing of child. She said that children were gift of god.

But, some advocates of social development, such as UN bureaucrats, privately fretted that Mother Teresa was the biggest stumbling block to the international family planning movement, bigger than America's "right-to life" movement.

Mother Teresa and the sisters continued opening houses all over India for caring for the poor, washing their wounds, and making them feel wanted. But her order's work spread across the world after 1965, when Pope Paul VI granted Mother Teresa's request to globally expand her order.

Whether it was in Ethiopia feeding the hungry, the ghettos of South Africa or it was her native country Macedonia, when the communist regime collapsed, Kolkata's Mother Teresa "the living saint" was there.

In 1982, at the height of the siege in Beirut, she convinced the parties to stop the war so that she could rescue 37 sick children trapped inside. Even war could not stop her works. Such daring works of her brought recognition throughout the world.

Mother Teresa became a symbol of untiring commitment to the poor and suffering. She was probably the most admired women of all time. She received many rewards and prizes for her outstanding work and she used her reputation travelling all over the world raising money and support for her causes.

— *** —

HER CHILDHOOD

The life history of Mother Teresa begins in Skopje, Macedonia in Eastern Europe. She was born on August 27, 1910 to a shopkeeper, Nikolle Bojaxhiu and his wife Drana of Albanian origin. Her parents settled in Skopje shortly after the beginning of the century.

The family always called her Gonxha, which means flower bud, because she was always plump, pink and cheerful. She was the youngest of three children, with a brother Lazar and sister Aga. They lived in a large house with a big garden.

Her parents were very caring and never turned away anyone who needed help. When Mother Teresa recalled her childhood she said 'We were a united and very happy family.' When Agnes was eight years old, her father died and the family was suddenly left in acute poverty.

Even in these conditions, she remembered her mother giving half their family meal to beggars who came to the gate, explaining to her three children, "They are our brothers and sisters. They are God's children." Her mother worked very hard to make sure the children were happy and Mother Teresa remembered her childhood as being 'exceptionally happy.'

As a public school student, she developed a special interest in overseas missions and, by age 12, realised her vocation was aiding the poor. She was given the name Agnes Gonxha.

The Bojaxhiu family, like many of their neighbours, was devout Roman Catholics. Religion played an important part in their lives; Mother Teresa recalled 'my mother taught us to love God and to love our neighbours.'

The little Agnes along with her sister took part in many church activities. Agnes loved to read about missionaries and about the lives of the saints. These influences brought much changes in her life.

Her brother Lazar recalled 'we lived next to the parish church of the Sacred Heart of Jesus. Sometimes my mother and sisters seemed to live as much in the church as they did at home. They were always involved with the choir, the religious services and missionary topics.'

Agnes took a particular interest in stories about missionaries in India and began to dream of becoming a missionary. When Agnes was 12 years old she believed that she heard God calling her to become a nun.

She talked to her mother and the local priest about this important decision. Agnes wanted to join it as soon as possible. But she had to wait for six years until she was eighteen and old enough to join a religious order. During this time of waiting she learnt about the Loreto nuns, sometimes known as the 'Irish Ladies.'

The Irish nuns were an international order of nuns founded in the sixteenth century. They set up schools in India and many other countries. Their services were known to all.

Agnes was not having good command over English language. In 1928, when she was only 18, Agnes travelled to Loreto Abbey in Ireland to learn English and began her life as a Loreto nun. Within a short span she garnered a great knowledge about nuns.

It must have been very hard for Agnes leaving home and going to a strange country to learn a new language. Although she had been brought up in a close loving family, she never saw her mother again. In later parts of her life, she expressed her love for her mother.

After just two months in Ireland she was sent on to the Loreto convent in Darjeeling in India. She continued to study English and started to learn Bengali, one of the Indian languages. She also began to learn how to live as a nun.

When she was 21, Agnes took her first vows. After taking her vows, she gave up the life she could have lived as Agnes Gonxha Bojaxhiu. She needed a new name for her new life, so she adopted the religious name Teresa. The person, who had been Agnes Bojaxhiu, was now Sister Teresa.

The new Sister Teresa was sent to teach geography and history at St. Mary's, a Loreto school in Kolkata, a big city in India. Many of the pupils were from wealthy homes. In 1937, she became the head teacher and took her final vows as a Loreto nun.

She knew she was doing a useful work and enjoyed teaching, but there were so many poor people outside the convent walls and she longed to help them. She could feel their worriness.

Whenever she could, she would go to the people of the slums with small gifts of food or medicines. This act brought her closer to the life of poor and destitute people. She always kept on thinking about them.

LIFE IN THE SLUMS

Very soon some changes were going to take place in the life of Sister Teresa. It was on September 10, 1946, after 17 happy years as a Loreto Sister, her life suddenly changed. Sister Teresa thought she heard the voice of God, she always remembered it as her 'day of inspiration'.

It was when Sister Teresa was quietly praying on a train travelling from Kolkata to Darjeeling, that God spoke to her. The powerful words of the God totally brought changes in her life.

From that day, she knew she must give up her safe and easy life in the convent to go and live with the poorest of the poor. She later recalled 'It was a command; I knew where I had to go.'

No sooner than later, Sister Teresa returned to the convent in Kolkata. Then she asked if she could leave to work in the slums. She had made up her mind in dedicating herself to the service of poor and specially needy people.

But unfortunately, the convent had different opinion. Living alone in the slums was considered far too dangerous and her request was refused. However, she had faith that if God wanted her to do this it would happen.

It took two years for Sister Teresa to get special permission from the Loreto Order to work in the slums. The Pope (the head of the Catholic Church) gave his blessing to her plans and Sister Teresa finally left the Loreto convent on August 16, 1948. She described this move into the slums as *'the most difficult thing I have ever done.'*

When she left the Loreto convent she gave up her dark nun's habit and dressed like a poor Indian woman in a simple white sari. The sari had a blue border to remind her of the Virgin Mary and she pinned a small cross to her left shoulder. She continued to wear this uniform for the rest of her life.

She realised that she would need medical skills to help the poor and spent four months on a short nursing course. Then on December 20, 1948, Sister Teresa went out for the first time by herself to work in the slums of Kolkata. From that day onwards, she worked for the slum people continously till her last breath.

Kolkata is one of the largest cities in the world. It is one of the world's most crowded cities. Rich and poor neighbourhoods exist next to each other. The slums were, and still are, terrible places. Life in the slums came as a great shock to Sister Teresa.

Many people had no homes; the lucky ones lived under old sacks. Many had only rags to wear, and hunger and disease were everywhere. There were constant nauseating smells of rotting garbage and sickness.

In fact, the situation at that time was at its worst. Old or sick people were left on the streets to die, eaten by rats and insects. Unwanted babies were thrown onto rubbish heaps.

She had just 5 rupees in her pocket when she went into the slums. She began by starting a school on the street. She made out a simple but workable plan to teach the people without much investment.

She used the dusty ground as her blackboard and a stick as her chalk. When people heard what she was doing, they sent gifts for her school. Thus day by day she brought changes in her teaching methods.

More and more people came to Sister Teresa for help. She worked very hard and she was very lonely. She wrote in her diary at the time — "Today, my God what tortures of loneliness. I wonder how long my heart will suffer this. Tears rolled and rolled. Everyone see my weakness. My God, give me courage now to fight self and the tempter. Let me not draw back from the sacrifice I have made of my free choice and conviction. Immaculate Heart of my Mother, have pity on thy poor child. For love of thee I want to live and die a Missionary of Charity."

Father Hardon Visits Mother Teresa's House of the Dying in Calcutta

However, other women who wanted to help the poor of Kolkata soon joined her. The Pope was so impressed with the work of Sister Teresa and her helpers that on October 7, 1950, he gave her permission to start a new order of nuns. She called her order 'The Congregation of the Missionaries of Charity.'

As the leader of this new order, Sister Teresa became Mother Teresa. In addition to the three vows all nuns take, the Missionaries of Charity added a new vow 'to give wholehearted, free service to the very poorest.' That vow played a very important role in the future course of action of the Missionary.

The tasks which the nuns were going to start were very pitiful. The nuns led a very simple life. They had very few possessions: Three saris, a pair of sandals, underwear, a crucifix, a bucket to wash in and a prayer book.

Each morning, the nuns woke up at 4:30 am to pray before going out to work in the slums. Some taught the children, some worked with the sick, the dying or those suffering from leprosy.

Mother Teresa worked alongside the other nuns not expecting them to do anything she would not do herself. Mother Teresa did not only want to help the dying, she wanted to help the living.

The slums were full of children needing help, so the Missionaries of Charity opened more schools, rescued unwanted babies and set up children's homes for abandoned or orphaned children. Mother Teresa said, "If you don't want a child give it to me."

The first home Mother Teresa opened was called

'Shishu Bhavan' which means the children's home. The children she took in were often filthy and covered in sores and lice. She and her nuns took them in, cleaned them and nursed them to health. Where possible, she tried to find loving homes for the children.

Another group desperately needing help were those suffering from leprosy, a terrible disease that deformed their bodies. Most people avoided any contact with people suffering from leprosy.

But Mother Teresa cared for them with loving kindness. In 1969, she started a leper village and called it 'Shanti Nagar' (The Place of Peace). The Missionaries of Charity also opened shelters to help disabled people. They were treated with love and affection.

Mother Teresa wanted to help poor people in other countries. The first home for the poor to be opened outside India was in Venezuela, in 1965. Today, Missionaries of Charity and their co-workers run more than 450 centres in over 100 countries to help the poor.

Running all these centres costs money. Mother Teresa had no money herself but she believed because it was God's work, that in some way God would provide the money. She was right; people from all over the world gave money to enable the work to continue.

For 19 years, the Missionaries of Charity helped thousands of poor people, but most ordinary people had never heard of them. In 1969, a British journalist,

Malcolm Muggeridge, from the BBC made a film about Mother Teresa and her work. It was called 'Something Beautiful for God'.

The film made Mother Teresa famous all over the world. Donations poured in to help her work and many people felt Mother Teresa's example changed their lives, including Malcolm Muggeridge himself. He said, 'She has given me a whole new vision of what being a Christian means.'

Malcolm Muggeridge believed his cameramen recorded an actual miracle taking place when they were filming in the house for the dying. No-one expected the scenes filmed in such dark rooms to come out; but when the film was processed everyone was amazed to find these scenes bathed in a beautiful soft light.

After the film was shown, her achievements were recognised around the world. She was given honorary degrees from a number of universities. Prizes and awards flooded in; when this included money she immediately spent it on the poor.

MOTHER IN KOLKATA

Kolkata, West Bengal's capital, holds a great position in the life of Mother Teresa. The dirt lane that led to Mother House from lower circular road back in those days is now paved over. Signs abound to guide the thousands who visit Mother Teresa's Missionaries of Charity headquarters in Kolkata today.

The Mother's simple tomb of white marble stands in the room in which she prayed with the sisters of her Order every morning. It is as unpretentious and simple as a room can be - like Mother herself, no matter who she was with.

Curious, sleepy young tourists with backpacks, the devout, those who believe they are walking in the footsteps of a saint, and those who knew her in the early days of her mission to help the poor, all trudge up the lane to pay Mother a visit, even though she is no longer with us — on the Earth.

She has made Kolkata famous, she has brought many tourists, and they love Mother. Her densely lined face looks out from framed photos in churches, doctor's and dentist's waiting rooms, clubs, schools and private homes, and her image even pops up beside garish

Bollywood posters pasted on city walls and railway stations.

Mother would have liked these juxtapositions. She would have beamed to see herself featured beside a Bollywood Romeo and Juliet. Mother loved happiness and love in all its forms.

Mother Teresa is a beloved icon in Kolkata, where she began her now famous order, The Missionaries of Charity. These Missionaries took a very important part in the beautification of the city's poor and sick children, elderly people and to those who were neglected by the people around them.

The Oxford Bookstore on Park Street has a table and several shelves devoted to the Nobel Peace Prize winner–now canonized a saint — whose name is synonymous with Kolkata, where she first began her mission.

When she died, she was laid in state at St. Thomas' Church, which is attached to the Loreto Convent at which she taught.

Mother Teresa spoke of one woman repeatedly at gatherings and meetings through the years, even after she won the Nobel Peace Prize in 1979. She described how she found her dying, abandoned in the gutters of a slum, infected with lice, TB and maggots.

When she was cleaning and changing the dying woman back at Nirmal Hriday — personally removing the maggots lodged in her flesh — she said the woman held her hand and said over and over again: "My family did this to me, they put me out of the house to die alone." The woman did not have long to live, but Mother personally attended to her.

It was the word "alone" that Mother zeroed in on when she spoke of this woman. She always emphasized "alone" and "unloved" so there was no mistaking their significance. "Make sure you look first to your own families to see that they are cared for and loved. Take care of your own, and there will be no poverty," Mother said often.

She always simplified life down to the essentials. Her speeches were never long or complicated and she had a delicious sense of humour. Her audiences could not feel bored of her speech, but would ask more and more.

Mother said she thought the elderly in the East were more fortunate than their counterparts in the West. She never understood putting parents in an "old people's home" or anything like that. It was a completely alien concept.

She worried about the homeless in a wealthy country like America, where she opened a home in the Bronx. She said the homeless in nations like Britain and America were more isolated and alone — and unloved — than the poor in India, who had so much company.

In India, wherever you look, there are poor people gravitating towards each other with a common bond — survival. Most homeless in the United States walk utterly alone — unloved.

Mother had such love and commitment for the marginalized and the stigmatized. Her relentless mission to improve the lot of lepers in India was life-long and meant a great deal to her. If she were alive now, she would be championing people living with the stigma of HIV/AIDS in India and around the world.

She would also be advocating to end the horror of *unmedicated* full-blown AIDS by giving those who cannot afford them the anti-retroviral medications *free*. The medications *exist,* but not for the poor. It is such a violation of human dignity and fundamental human rights.

Dignity for the outcast, the forgotten and abandoned was vitally important to Mother, but this was not easy to communicate when there was so much poverty in India.

Mother did not believe in "untouchability." For her, how people treated others was a test of their "humanity." Those who walked beside Mother would by necessity have to walk where the shunned and the outcast dwelled. They would have to risk controversy and censure.

Mother Teresa's moral bar was one of her own creation. But she did not impose it on anyone, except by the extraordinary example she set in her daily life.

Mother Teresa is synonymous to forgiveness in a way. She had no recriminations for those who could not walk her road. Mother's strength came from her deep faith, which nothing — not even the worst atrocities she witnessed — could erode.

For all of those who knew her then, she will always be "Mother." She walked where few dare to tread and she witnessed her fellow human beings at their lowest possible ebb.

Mother Teresa would be always there to those in grief. She found and inspired hope in the most degraded circumstances. She never tired and she never recoiled from what she found.

She believed in helping, and in healing, even if the person had only a few hours to live. She only tried to ease their tension and mental agony. Thereby they could go to the heaven happily.

BEATIFICATION

It was finally on October 19, 2003, that Pope John Paul II celebrated the ancient ritual of the Catholic Church in St. Peter's Square, Rome, to beatify Mother Teresa of Kolkata. What made this occasion unique was that John Paul II knew Mother Teresa personally, and that she died only a few years ago.

Infact Mother Teresa was the most admired Catholic of the 20 century. It was due to her heroic work on behalf of the poorest of the poor, a work which began when she began caring for the destitute and dying in the gutters of Kolkata over 50 years ago and her service to the mankind all over the world.

Her endless contributions to the world of poor and destitutes are still carrying out through her Missionary. The religious order which she founded in 1948 has since spread throughout the world, has over 4,000 members, and has many centres to assist the poor, lepers, the elderly, the blind, and people living with AIDS.

Mother Teresa also opened schools and homes for the poor and abandoned children. She is regarded as a national treasure in India, the nation where she became a citizen, and in her home country, Macedonia, where some 70 percent of the population are Muslims. These schools and homes gave a very different life to lead to the poor and abandoned children.

In the normal process, a period of five years must elapse after a person's death for the commencement of the process, which leads to beatification. However, the Holy Father waived this, and the process began two years after Mother Teresa entered eternal life.

In October 2002, the Congregation for the Causes of Saints recognized as authentic a miracle attributed to Mother Teresa of Kolkata, thereby passing one of the conditions for beatification. It was unbelievable but it had exactly happened.

The miracle occurred on September 5, 1998, just a year after Mother Teresa's death. A 30-year-old woman, Monica Besra, a non-Christian woman from Kolkata, was near death with a large abdominal tumour.

She visited the Missionaries of Charity, to pray for her life, for a miracle. She told CNN, *"As soon as I stepped into the church, there was a photograph of Mother Teresa, and there was a light from the photograph that came toward me and I was stunned. Later, the sisters prayed for me, and I went to sleep. When I got up at 1 in the morning, I found the big tumour had disappeared."*

Surprisingly, the young woman had experienced a complete and immediate cure. Her doctor, Dr R.N.

Bhattacharya, also a non-Christian, said, "I did not find any reason that without an operation a tumour of such size would disappear overnight."

He further added, "It is difficult to describe what I felt with this whole event. But this is one of the most wonderful experiences that I ever had in my medical career."

An exhaustive investigation by the Congregation, backed by expert medical and scientific testimony, confirmed the miracle. Finally, they had to admit the miracle of Mother.

What made Mother Teresa so widely admired, and loved, was that she saw Jesus in even the most distressing situations, and in her own life, fulfilled in the most radical way Jesus' teaching, "Whenever you do this to even the least of my brethren, you do it to me."

Her work became very widely known in the West, as a result of a book *Something Beautiful for God,* written by the well-known writer and commentator, Malcolm Muggeridge. Indeed, Muggeridge's own conversion to the Catholic faith was probably due to his contact with Mother Teresa.

For many people Mother Teresa was a saint on earth, a powerful force for good. Others disagreed with her ideas, they criticised her for accepting money from anyone, even criminals. Some said she should have run her homes differently and others complained she was too controlling.

The Catholic Church may or may not declare her to be a saint. What is true is that millions of people are grateful for the difference she made to their lives. And there is no other way to prove her other than these people.

In her support, many famous and well known people came forward. As the journalist Mary Kenny wrote in the Independent 'Even her bitterest critics cannot deny that ... she did indeed accomplish something beautiful for God.'

CATHOLIC TEACHINGS

Mother Teresa had done something which no one could equal her. Her heroic life was also lived in complete conformity to the teachings of the Catholic faith, and she gave a marvellous example of this fidelity on issues like contraception and abortion.

She could even go against any of the world bodies if they differ with her. When bodies such as the UN were demanding that India implement draconian birth control policies to restrict India's population growth, Mother Teresa insisted that children were gifts from God, and should always be welcomed.

After East Bengal broke away from Pakistan to form Bangladesh, Pakistani troops invaded the country, in the course of which many thousands of young Bengali women were raped, making them outcasts.

Although international aid agencies offered free abortions, Mother Teresa began a unique programme by offering complete care for the young women, describing them as heroes, and helping many to have their babies. It was necessary, she said, to "fight abortion with adoption." She strongly propagated about it to the whole nation through her teaching.

"It was so wonderful to see the greatness of that man who could speak like that without blaming anybody, without comparing anything, like an angel. This is the greatness of people who are spiritually rich even when they are materially poor."

Her beatification is a major step on the path to canonisation, when she is declared to be a saint. That happy event will occur when one further miracle, positively attributable to her intervention, is authenticated.

THE FINAL YEARS

It was in 1990 that the health of Mother Teresa became worse. She was suffering from heart trouble and wanted to resign as the head of the Missionaries of Charity. She was almost 80 years old.

Even though, Mother Teresa was old and weak, no one could carry on the work with the same energy as she did. The Missionaries of Charity insisted no one could take her place. Finally she accepted the proposal and so she continued.

Mother Teresa's health was deteriorating, partly from age, part from the conditions where she was living, and part of it was from her trips all over the world, opening new houses and raising money for the poor.

In 1985, she had a heart attack while in Rome visiting Pope John Paul II. Afterwards such life taking attacks were frequented. In short, her final day was approaching.

In 1989, she suffered another almost fatal heart attack and had a pacemaker implanted. In 1991, she caught pneumonia in Tijuana, Mexico, which lead to heart failure. She had in her mind a lot of tasks to carry out before she bade final goodbye to the rest of the people on earth.

In 1996, Mother Teresa caught malaria as well as chest infection and had heart surgery. These treatments almost weakened her health further. But in March 1997, Mother Teresa became too weak to carry on as head of the Missionaries of Charity. She was looking for a substitute. Finally 63-year-old Sister Nirmala was chosen to take her place.

Sister Nirmala refused to take the title of 'Mother' for 'No one can ever replace Mother Teresa' she said. However, she and the other Missionaries of Charity vow to continue to serve the poorest of the poor.

Now came the very unfortunate day for mankind. On September 5, 1997, Mother Teresa died. All her life she had been inspired by Jesus' words 'Love one another as I have loved you.' These words are carved on her grave.

Her loss is irreparable. Mother Teresa's funeral was held at the Netaji Indoor Stadium in India, which holds 15,000 people.

At the insistence of the Missionaries of Charity, half of the seats were reserved for the poor and sick that Mother Teresa took care of during her life. This indicated the place of the poor and sick people in the heart of Mother Teresa.

The State Funeral services usually reserved for Heads of State were led by Cardinal Sodano; the Vatican's secretary of state and the Pope's representative.

Among the people attending Mother Teresa's funeral were Hillary Clinton, representing the US, Bernadette Chirac for France, Italy's Prime Minister Oscar Luigi, Canada's Deputy Prime Minister Peter Jennings, Albania's President Rexhep Mejdani, Ghana's President Jerry Rawlings, the Duchess of Kent represented the British Monarchy, Queen Noor of Jordan, Queen Sofia of Spain, and Queen Fabiola of Belgium.

Even with Mother Teresa gone, her sisters at the Missionaries of Charities still strive to realize Mother Teresa's dream of a world where everyone has a home where they can be loved and cared for.

— *** —

AWARDS

Mother Teresa was recognized all over the world and she received many awards all of which are as follows.

In 1962, she received The *Magsaysay Award* for International Understanding along with a cheque of 50,000 rupees. She used this award money to buy the Children's Home in Agra.

In 1962, she also received India's second highest award the '*Padma Shri*', from the President of India, Dr. Rajendra Prasad.

In January 1971, Pope Paul VI presented her with a cheque worth £10,000 given by the Vatican as the first *Pope John XXIII Peace Prize*. She received the cheque and donated it for the construction of a leper colony in Madhya Pradesh on land donated by the Indian Government.

On October 13, of the same year Joseph P. Kennedy Jr. Foundation presented her with an award in Washington. The award was made up of a heavy glass vase engraved with a figure of St. Raphael the Archangel and inscribed with the increasingly familiar words : "*To Mother Teresa, whose struggles have shaped something beautiful for God.*"

In November 1972, she was given the *Nehru Award* for international understanding by the Indian government. The Award consisted of a citation describing her as "*one of the most impressive manifestations of charity throughout the world*". It stated further that she had inspired a large number of devoted people all over the world to work with her in the service of the destitute, the uncared and helpless people of the society.

In 1973, Mother Teresa was awarded the *Templeton Prize* for Progress in Religion, which made her the first recipient of this Prize. She was selected out of a total of two thousand nominations by a panel of judges representing the major religious traditions of the world, including Christianity, Judaism, Buddhism and Hinduism.

In 1974, the Prime Minister of the Yemen Arab Republic presented her with a *'Sword of Honour'*.

In March 1975, the United Nations Food and Agriculture Organization struck its *Ceres Medals* in recognition of Mother's *"exemplary love and concern for the hungry and the poorest of the poor"*. The Medal showed Mother Teresa representing the Roman Goddess of Agriculture.

In June 1975, Mother Teresa was awarded the *Voice of America's International Women's Year Pin* for her work for the poor in India.

On October 23, 1975, she became a recipient of one of the first *Albert Schweitzer* International Prizes, awarded at the University of North Carolina, Washington.

On November 2, 1975, she was awarded an honorary Doctor of Laws degree, at a special ceremony at St. Francis Xavier University in Antigonish, Nova Scotia. In the same year (*International Women's Year*), Shirley Williams, the then Secretary of State for Consumer Protection in the British government, and Maurice Strong, executive director of The United Nations Environment Program, Senator Edward Kennedy and

Robert McNamara, head of the World Bank, added their support to the nomination of Mother Teresa for the Nobel Peace Prize.

On March 3, 1976, Mrs. Indira Gandhi, as chancellor of the Vishwa Bharti University, conferred on Mother Teresa the University's highest honour, *The Deshikottama* (Doctor of Literature) scarf in recognition of her significant contribution to the cause of human suffering. Mrs. Gandhi commented on her, *"She is tiny to look at, but there is nothing small about her."*

In June 1977, she was awarded an honorary *Doctorate of Divinity* from the University of Cambridge. On October 17, 1979, she was awarded the *Nobel Peace Prize* with a cheque for $130,000.

On December 8, 1979, Mother Teresa landed at Oslo's international airport accompanied by Sister Agnes and Sister Gertrude. She had politely refused the heavy coats and fur-lined boots to protect against a temperature of minus ten degrees Celsius offered to her by the Nobel committee.

She requested cancellation of the celebratory banquet and said that the money should be used for those who were really in need of a meal. Thus, the $4,000 that was to be spent for the banquet and further $50,000 raised by Norwegian young people were added to her prize money. More than one thousand people welcomed her.

The Indian Ambassador in Norway gave her a reception the moment she landed at Oslo. She was grateful for the prize, as it would provide housing for the homeless and for leper families. Moreover, she was especially grateful for the *"gift of recognition of the poorest of the poor of the world"*.

Mother Teresa was awarded the Nobel Prize "for work undertaken in the struggle to overcome poverty and distress, which also constitute a threat to peace." When Mother Teresa received the prize, she was asked, "What can we do to promote world peace?" Her answer was simple: "Go home and love your family."

When she heard the news of Nobel Prize, she replied 'I accept this award in the name of the poor.' World leaders answered her calls because they recognised her compassion for others.

During the Ethiopian famine of 1981 she wrote to the US President Reagan. He promised to do everything possible to help and the government rushed in with food and medicine.

Both Prince Charles and Diana, Princess of Wales visited Mother Teresa and were greatly impressed by her work.

On December 10, 1979, in the presence of King Olaf V of Norway, Crown Prince Harald, Crown Princess Sonja, and many other dignitaries, Mother Teresa accepted the gold medal and the money, as she had accepted all other honours, *'unworthily'* but *"gratefully in the name of poor, the hungry, the sick and the lonely"*.

The Indian Government further honoured her in 1980, as she became one of the only three Indian nationals ever to receive a Nobel Prize. She was also one of the only three Indians ever to have been honoured with an official reception within the ramparts of Delhi's historic Red Fort. The other two recipients were Jawaharlal Nehru and his daughter Indira Gandhi.

In the Rashtrapati Bhavan, the Presidential Palace in New Delhi, the President of India, Neelam Sanjiva Reddy, gave her India's highest civilian award, the *'Bharat Ratna'* or *'Jewel of India'*.

In the same year she was awarded the gold medal of the official Soviet Peace Committee.

On November 24, 1983, Queen Elizabeth II at the Presidential Palace in Delhi presented Mother Teresa with the insignia of the Honorary Order of Merit.

On June 20, 1985, at the White House in Washington, the then US President, Ronald Reagan presented her with the United States Presidential Medal of Freedom, calling her a *'heroine of our times'*. He declared that *"the goodness in some hearts transcends all borders and all narrow nationalistic considerations"*.

On October 27 of the same year, she was honoured at the National Shrine of the Immaculate Conception in Washington, when Cardinal O'Boyle, Chairman of the

Shrine's Committee, presented her with a monetary gift on behalf of the thousand of visitors to the Shrine.

On July 1987, the film 'Mother Teresa' made by two American sisters, Ann and Jeanette Petric, was awarded the Soviet Peace Committee Prize during the 15th International Film Festival held in Moscow.

On March 28, Yasser Arafat, President of the Palestine Liberation organization, presented her with a cheque of US $50,000. He invited her to the Holy Land and asked her to open 'Death with Dignity' homes in Bethlehem and Jerusalem.

In August 1992, in New York, she received the Knights of St. Columbanus' *Gaudium et Spes* (Hope and Joy) Award from Cardinal John O' Connor.

On August 1992, she was awarded with an honorary fellowship of the Royal College of Surgeons in Ireland.

On December 1992, in Kolkata, she received the United Nations cultural agency's peace education award to *"crown a life consecrated to the service of the poor, to the promotion of peace and to combating injustice"*. The UNESCO director general presented her a cheque of £50,000. The money was used by her to set up a home for the handicapped near Kolkata.

In the same year, the communist President of Albania, Mr. Ramiz Alia, awarded Albanian citizenship to Mother Teresa, who had once been forced to take a sad decision of not visiting her dying mother in her homeland, as she wanted to serve the poor of the world. Mr. Alia also created a *'Mother Teresa Prize'* to be awarded to those who distinguished themselves in the field of humanitarian and charitable work.

In January 1993, she received the papal award '*Pro Ecclesia et Pontifice*'.

In October 1994, she received the *'U Thant Peace Award'* for her 'Tireless Service to humanity'.

On May 16, 1997, she was awarded a United States Congressional gold medal in recognition of her "outstanding and enduring contributions to humanitarian and charitable activities".

WORDS OF THE MOTHER

On poverty

"I see God in every human being. When I wash the leper's wounds, I feel I am nursing the Lord himself. Is it not a beautiful experience?" — 1974 interview.

"When I see waste here, I feel angry on the inside. I don't approve of myself getting angry. But it's something you can't help after seeing Ethiopia." — Washington 1984.

On the Nobel Peace Prize

"I choose the poverty of our poor people. But I am grateful to receive (the Nobel) in the name of the hungry, the naked, the homeless, of the crippled, of the blind, of the lepers, of all those people who feel unwanted, unloved, uncared-for throughout society, people that have become a burden to the society and are shunned by everyone." — Accepting the Nobel Peace Prize, 1979.

On war

"I have never been in a war before, but I have seen famine and death. I was asking (myself), 'What do they feel when they do this?' I don't understand it. They are all children of God. Why do they do it? I don't understand." — Beirut 1982, during fighting between the Israeli army and Palestinian guerrillas.

"Please choose the way of peace. ... In the short term there may be winners and losers in this war that we all dread. But that never can, nor never will justify the suffering, pain and loss of life your weapons will cause." — Letter to US President George Bush and Iraqi President Saddam Hussein, January 1991.

On loving, caring and abortion

"Jesus died on the Cross because that is what it took for Him to do good to us —to save us from our selfishness in sin. He gave up everything to do the Father's will —to show us that we too must be willing to give up everything to do God's will —to love one another as He loves each of us. That is why we too must give to each other until it hurts.

It is not enough for us to say: "I love God," but I also have to love my neighbour. St. John says that you are a liar if you say you love God and you don't love your neighbour. How can you love God whom you do not see, if you do not love your neighbour whom you see, whom you touch, with whom you live? And so it is very important for us to realize that love, to be true, has to hurt. I must be willing to give whatever it takes not to harm other people and, in fact, to do good to them. This requires that I be willing to give until it hurts. Otherwise, there is no true love in me and I bring injustice, not peace, to those around me.

It hurt Jesus to love us. We have been created in His image for greater things, to love and to be loved. We just "put on Christ" as Scripture tells us. And so, we have been created to love as He loves us. Jesus makes Himself the hungry one, the naked one, the homeless one, the unwanted one, and He says, "You did it unto Me." On the last day He will say to those on His right, "whatever you did to the least of these, you did to Me, and He will also say to those on His left, whatever you neglected to do for the least of these, you neglected to do it for Me."

When He was dying on the Cross, Jesus said, "I thirst". Jesus is thirsting for our love, and this is the thirst of everyone, poor or rich alike. We all thirst for the love of others, that they will go out of their way to avoid harming us and to do good to us. This is the meaning of truest love, to give until it hurts.

I can never forget the experience I had in visiting a home where they kept all these old parents of sons and daughters who had just put them into an institution and forgotten them —maybe. I saw that in that home these old people had everything —good food, comfortable place, television, everything, but everyone was looking toward the door. And I did not see a single one with a smile on the face. I turned to Sister and I asked: "Why do these people who have every comfort here, why are they all looking towards the door? Why are they not smiling?"

I am so used to seeing the smiles on our people, even the dying ones smile. And Sister said: "This is the way it is nearly every day. They are expecting, they are hoping that a son or daughter will come to visit them. They are hurt because they are forgotten." And see, this neglect to love brings spiritual poverty. Maybe in our own family we have somebody who is feeling lonely, who is feeling sick, who is feeling worried. Are we there?

Are we willing to give until it hurts in order to be with our families, or do we put our own interests first? These are the questions we must ask ourselves, especially as we begin this year of the family. We must remember that love begins at home and we must also remember that the future of humanity passes through the family.

I was surprised in the West to see so many young boys and girls given to drugs. And I tried to find out why. Why is it like that, when those in the West have so many more things than those in the East? And the answer was: Because there is no one in the family to receive them.

Our children depend on us for everything —their health, their nutrition, their security, their coming to know and love God. For all of this, they look to us with trust, hope and expectation. But often father and mother are so busy they have no time for their children, or perhaps they are not even married or have given up on marriage. So the children go to the streets and get involved in drugs and other things.

But I feel that the greatest destroyer of peace today is abortion, because it is a war against the child, a direct killing of the innocent child, murder by the mother herself. And if we accept that a mother can kill even her own child, how can we tell other people not to kill one another? How do we persuade a woman not to have an abortion? As always, we must persuade her with love and we remind ourselves that love means willing to give until it hurts. Jesus gave even His life to love us. So, the mother who is thinking of abortion, should be helped to love, that is, to give until it hurts her plans, or her free time, to respect the life of her child. The father of that child, whoever he is, must also give until it hurts.

By abortion, the mother does not learn to love, but kills even her own child to solve her problems. And, by abortion, the father is told that he does not have to take any responsibility at all for the child he has brought into the world. That father is likely to put other women into the same trouble. So abortion just leads to more abortion. Any country that accepts abortion is not teaching its people to love, but to use any violence to get what they want. This is why the greatest destroyer of love and peace is abortion.

Many people are very, very concerned with the children of India, with the children of Africa where quite a few die of hunger, and so on. Many people are also concerned about all the violence in this great country of the United States. But often these same people are not concerned with the millions who are being killed by the deliberate decision of their own mothers. And this is what is the greatest destroyer of peace today — abortion which brings people to such blindness.

And for this I appeal in India and I appeal everywhere, "Let us bring the child back." The child is God's gift to the family. Each child is created in the special image and likeness of God for greater things — to love and to be loved. In this year of the family, we must bring the child back to the centre of our care and concern. This is the only way that our world can survive because our children are the only hope for the future. As older people are called to God, only their children can take their place.

But what does God say to us? He says: "Even if a mother could forget her child, I will not forget you. I have carved you in the palm of my hand." We are carved in the palm of His hand; that unborn child has been carved in the hand of God from conception and is called by God to love and to be loved, not only now in this life, but forever. God can never forget us.

I will tell you something beautiful. We are fighting abortion by adoption —by care of the mother and adoption for her baby. We have saved thousands of lives. We have sent word to the clinics, to the hospitals, and to the police stations: "Please don't destroy the child; we will take the child." So we always have someone tell the mothers in trouble: "Come, we will take care of you, we will get a home for your child." And we have a tremendous demand from couples who cannot have a child —but I never give a child to a couple who have done something not to have a child. Jesus said, " Anyone who receives a child in my name, receives me." By adopting a child, these couples receive Jesus but, by aborting a child, a couple refuses to receive Jesus.

Please don't kill the child. I want the child. Please give me the child. I am willing to accept any child who would be aborted and to give that child to a married couple who will love the child and be loved by the child. From our children's home in Kolkata alone, we have saved over 3,000 children from abortion. These children have brought such love and joy to the adopting parents and have grown up so full of love and joy.

I know that couples have to plan their family and for that there is natural family planning. The way to plan the family is natural family planning, not contraception. In destroying the power of giving life, through contraception, a husband or wife is doing something to self. This turns the attention to self and so it destroys the gift of love in him or her. In loving, the husband and wife must turn the attention to each other as happens in natural family planning, and not to self, as happens in contraception. Once that living love is destroyed by contraception, abortions follows very easily.

I also know that there are great problems in the world —that many spouses do not love each other enough to practice natural family planning. We cannot solve all the problems in the world, but let us never bring in the worst problem of all, and that is to destroy love. And this is what happens when we tell people to practice contraception and abortion.

The poor are very great people. They can teach us so many beautiful things. Once one of them came to thank us for teaching her natural family planning because it is nothing more than self-control out of love for each other. And what this poor person said is very true. These poor people maybe have nothing to eat, maybe they have not a home to live in, but they can still be great people when they are spiritually rich.

When I pick up a person from the street, hungry, I give him a plate of rice, a piece of bread. But a person who is shut out, who feels unwanted, unloved, terrified, the person who has been thrown out of society —that spiritual poverty is much harder to overcome. And abortion, which often follows from contraception, brings a people to be spiritually poor, and that is the worst poverty and the most difficult to overcome.

We are not social workers. We may be doing social work in the eyes of some people, but we must be contemplatives in the heart of the world. For we must bring that presence of God into your family, for the family that prays together, stays together. There is so much hatred, so much misery, and we with our prayer, with our sacrifice, are beginning at home. Love begins at home, and it is not how much we do, but how much love we put into what we do.

If we are contemplatives in the heart of the world with all its problems, these problems can never discourage us. We must always remember what God tells us in Scripture: "even if a mother could forget the child in her womb —something impossible, but even if she could forget —I will never forget you."

And so here I am talking to you. I want you to find the poor here, right in your own home first. And begin love there. Be that good news to your own people first. And find out about your next-door neighbours. Do you know who they are?

I had the most extraordinary experience of love of neighbour with a Hindu family. A gentleman came to our house and said, "Mother Teresa, there is a family who have not eaten for so long. Do something." So I took some rice and went there immediately. And I saw the children —their eyes shining with hunger. I don't know if you have ever seen hunger. But I have seen it very often. And the mother of the family took the rice I gave her and went out.

When she came back, I ask her: "Where did you go? What did you do?" And she gave me a very simple answer: "They are hungry also." What struck me was that she knew —and who are they? A Muslim family — and she knew. I didn't bring any more rice that evening because I wanted them, Hindus and Muslims, to enjoy the joy of sharing.

But there were those children, radiating joy, sharing the joy and peace with their mother because she had the love to give until it hurts. And you see this is where love begins —at home in the family.

So, as the example of this family shows, God will never forget us and there is something you and I can always do. We can keep the joy of loving Jesus in our hearts, and share that joy with all we come into contact with. Let us make that one point —that no child will be unwanted, unloved, uncared for, or killed and thrown away. And give until it hurts —with a smile.

Because I talk so much of giving with a smile, once a professor from the United States asked me, "Are you married:" And I said, "Yes, and I find it sometimes very difficult to smile at my spouse, Jesus, because He can be very demanding —sometimes."

One of the most demanding things for me is travelling everywhere— and with publicity. I had said to Jesus that if I don't go to heaven for anything else, I will be going to heaven for all the travelling with all the publicity, because it has purified me and sacrificed me and made me really ready to go to heaven.

If we remember that God loves us, and that we can love others as He loves us, then America can become a sign of peace for the world.

From here, a sign of care for the weakest of the weak —the unborn child— must go out to the world. If you become a burning light of justice and peace in the world, then really you will be truest to what the founders of this country stood for. God bless you!

On retirement

"God will find another person, more humble, more devoted, more obedient to him, and the society will go on." — Kolkata 1989, after announcing her intention to retire.

"I was expecting to be free, but God has his own plans." — Kolkata 1990, when the sisters of her order persuaded her to withdraw her resignation.

ON HER LIFE'S WORK

It's a story of around 50 years ago, Mother Teresa found a woman "half eaten by maggots and rats" lying in front of a Kolkata hospital. The diminutive Roman Catholic nun sat with the woman until she died.

In no time, she began a campaign for a shelter for people to die with dignity. Until her death, she made a mission of caring for the human castoffs the world wanted to forget. Such enduring task needed strong dedication.

Mother, with great effort, created a global network of homes for the poor, from the hovels of Kolkata to the ghettos of New York, including one of the first homes for AIDS victims. Since AIDS were and still are spreading like a wild fire among the youths, either in India or Western countries and African countries.

Poverty and homelessness had a formidable and unrelenting foe in Mother Teresa. It was whether in Ethiopia tending to the hungry or in the squalid townships of South Africa, Kolkata's "angel of mercy" was there. She could not ignore all such problems of the helplessness of the citizens of the world.

People always praised her works and contributions. But her funding methods met with some criticism. Mother Teresa's causes were financed by public foundations, private donors and scores of prizes. Inspite of such financial burden, she continued her work continously.

It was in 1994, a British television documentary, "Hell's Angel: Mother Teresa of Kolkata," accused her of accepting contributions without questioning the source, including the likes of Haitian dictator Jean-Claude Duvalier.

Who ever blamed her, had to shut their mouth with the decent reply of her. Mother Teresa had a short response to such allegations: "No matter who says what, you should accept it with a smile and do your own work," she said.

Under Mother Teresa's guidance, the order focused much of its attention on giving comfort to the dying, a task the sisters continue. In an abandoned temple to the Hindu goddess Kali, Mother Teresa founded the Kalighat Home for the Dying. To Mother, there was no level of religion to the poor people.

After the Kalighat Home, the order had another focus of expanding their works. The order established Shanti Nagar (Town of Peace), a leper colony, in the mid-1950s on land granted from the Indian government.

Mainly in India and beyond, Mother Teresa and her Missionaries of Charity devoted their time to the blind, the disabled, the aged, and the poor. How much these neglected people needed Mother!

She opened schools, orphanages and homes for the needy, and turned her attention to the victims of AIDS as that disease increased in prevalence. By 1996, she was operating 517 missions in more than 100 countries.

And she did ... returning to work time and again after serious health setbacks. Following a nearly fatal heart attack in 1990, Mother Teresa announced her intention to resign as head of her order.

But in the following days, an interesting incident took place in the life of Mother. During a secret ballot of her sisters, she was re-elected almost unanimously. In fact she was the most deserving to hold the position.

Mother Teresa was not only a worker of love but also a speaker and teacher of love. Wherever she went, she spoke on her work as well as on issues related to her work.

www.ingramcontent.com/pod-product-compliance
Lightning Source LLC
LaVergne TN
LVHW051203080426
835508LV00021B/2785